The MOON
& the MONTH

A Fatwa on the Importance of Sighting
the Crescent for Determining
the Lunar Months

By
Shaykh al-Islam of Africa
AL-HAJJ IBRAHIM NIASSE

Introduction by
Shaykh Hassan Cisse

Translation by
Talut Dawood

First published in 2019 by Fayda Books, Publishing & Distribution 2690 Campbellton Rd.

http://www.faydabooks.com

Email: orders@faydabooks.com

© Copyright Fayda Books 2019

ISBN 978-1-7339631-1-4

No part of this book may be reproduced in any form without prior permission of the publishers. All rights reserved.

Cover design and typeset by Muhammadan Press

Printed and bound in the United States

Thanks to Imam Cheikh Tidiane Cisse for the permission to translate, publish and print all works pertaining to Islam, Tariqa Tijaniyya and Fayda.

CONTENTS

Publisher's Preface	7
Prologue by the Shaykh and Imam	9
Foreword	11
An Investigation of the Necessity of Sighting the *Hilal*	13
Biography of the Author	31

PUBLISHER'S PREFACE

It is with great pleasure that we present to you, a legal verdict (*Fatwa*) on one of the most controversial issues that has caused division and anxiety in the community of Muslims worldwide. This problem usually rears its head immediately before the start of the holy month of Ramadan and reaches its apex towards the end of the holy month. Each faction giving its own reasoning as to how it derives its formula for starting the month and ending it. The groups that adhere to the pronouncements of Saudi Arabia as to when to begin and end fasting are there. We also find the groups that adhere to their ancestral home sightings. Then there are the groups that prefer to use scientific calculations to derive their start and ending dates. Finally, there are the groups who chose to follow the local sightings of trusted community members or fatwa councils.

The translation of this important evaluation of what the Holy Quran and Noble Sunnah says about sighting the Hilal (New Crescent Moon) of a month, is long overdue. Shaykh Ibrahim Niasse masterfully brings forth all of the proofs and reasoning necessary to bring this contentious issue to rest. We pray that it serves as a guide for all who are interested in knowing the truth by the TRUTH.

We added a short biography of Shaykh Ibrahim Niasse at the end of the treatise. Islamic scholars of West Africa have long been ignored or overlooked when it comes to the mastery of their knowledge in all of the fields of the Islamic sciences. We hope this book will induce true seekers of knowledge to further investigate the incredible literary and scholarly brilliance of this man of Allah.

Wasalaam
Ibrahim A. Dimson
Publisher, Fayda Books

PROLOGUE BY THE SHAYKH AND IMAM HASSAN CISSE
(ALLAH HAVE MERCY ON HIM AND BE PLEASED WITH HIM)[1]

All praise is due to Allah who *"taught by the pen; He taught man what he did not know"* [AL-'ALAQ, 4-5]. And may prayers and blessings be upon the noblest of the Messengers, our Master Muhammad, who said, *"If anyone travels a path in which he seeks knowledge, Allah will make easy for him one of the paths that lead to Paradise."* He also said, *"The Angels lower their wings to the seeker of knowledge out of satisfaction with his action."* He also said, *"All those in the heavens and the earth seek, even the whales in the sea, seek forgiveness for the scholar."* He also said, *"The superiority of the scholar over the worshipper is like the superiority of the moon to the stars."* And he said, *"The scholars are the heirs of the Prophets. The Prophets don't bequeath gold or silver. Rather, they only bequeath knowledge. So, if anyone takes it, he has taken an ample portion."* And may blessings and peace be upon his family and companions, the guided guides, as well as the generation that followed them, and all those who follow them in excellence until the Day of Judgement.

We are happy to present, to the lovers of the Shaykh—Shaykh al-Islam al-Hajj Ibrahim Niasse, *may Allah be pleased with him, cause him to be satisfied and be pleased with us on his behalf. Amin.* This important compilation, from among his prestigious works. It has been republished with the intention of keeping his legacy alive and out of eagerness to benefit and remind the believers. Allah (Exalted is He) has said: *"And remind. Indeed, reminders benefit*

---

[1] In the original text, the supplications *"May Allah perpetuate his honor and extend his life"* were used. The Shaykh has passed since the last printing of this book. So, I thought it more appropriate to use the formulas for the pious who have passed on.

the believers" [AL-DHARIYAT, 55]. Furthermore, there is no doubt that we are in need of listening to the voice of the Shaykh in all matters or reading his ingenious points of view on a variety of topics. This is especially the case in this time. Since he has not left us neglected, it is imperative, at every moment, that we review his precious and priceless writings through reading and discussion. That is because they all adhere to the Book and the Sunnah. And we are doubly in need of extracting lessons and benefitting form them inwardly and outwardly.

Thus, I present to you that which I am able in the time, hoping from Allah (*Blessed and Exalted is He*) that He make it possible for us to publish for the first time whatever has not been published and reprint anything that is scarce in the bookstores. For, He is the illuminated lamp for us in our journey to the Real (*Majestic is His affair*). And He is the Straight Path. If anyone holds tight to him, he is guided. And if anyone seeks refuge in him, they are saved. May Allah enable us and you to that in which there is benefit for Islam and the Muslims.

We thank all those who helped to make this work possible and facilitated this sublime effort. And we ask Allah that He reward them, on our behalf, with much good. And may He make theirs and our feet firm. And the last of our prayers is that all praise is for Allah, Lord of all the worlds. Peace

(Shaykh) Al-Hassan ʿAli Cisse
Madinah Kaolack
3rd of Shawwal 1416 AH
25th of February, 1996 CE

FOREWORD

All praise is due to Allah by whose grace good works are completed. May blessings and peace be upon our Master Muhammad, who said, *"Fast when you see it. And break your fast when you see it."* And may blessings and peace be upon his pure family and elect companions, as well as all those who follow them in excellence until the Day of Judgement.

To proceed:

This book is one of dozens of books written by the honorable Shaykh al-Islam and guide of mankind, the custodian of the sanctuary of the Muhammadan creed, about whom the scholars of his age testified to his vast knowledge and wise reading, and to whom the Saints of his age, the Shaykh of Shaykhs, the mine of steadfastness, the Imam of the guided Imams, the Seal of the realized folk, the support of the *Qutbs* and Gnostics, the spiritual educator of the possessors of intellect, children of gnosis and certainty, our Master and Support, our Shaykh, Mawlana Shaykh Ibrahim b. al-Hajj Abdullah Niasse al-Kawlakhi al-Senegali al-Tijani (*may Allah be pleased with him*) (1320-1395 AH).

This book, if it is small in form and length, it comprises much assistance and great benefit, resolving one of the issues in Islam of great importance to the Muslims. Indeed, I am referring to the issue of sighting the *hilal* and the Muslims being united upon the start and end of the fast in the Islamic world, to which some have called. The Shaykh has taken a definitive stance in the matter, which is clear to the reader of the book. That stance is completely entrenched in the Book and the Sunnah. And the Shaykh has clarified, in this book, that it is impossible for the Muslims to be united in the start and end of their fast. In that, he depended upon both textual and intellectual evidence. And he consolidated his proof with authentic evidences from the Book and the Sunnah and the opinions of the notable scholars, as was his habit. Thus, his book became a perfect, curative compendium, the best resource of the subject on which to rely, until, very soon after the publication of the Shaykh's book, the legal verdicts of the fiqh councils all coincided with the opinion of the Shaykh. Thus, Allah benefited the *Ummah* by it and gave victory to the Sunnah. Peace.

The Publisher
7th of Shawwal 1416 AH
27th of February 1996

AN INVESTIGATION OF THE NECESSITY OF SIGHTING THE HILAL

By the pen of Shaykh al-Islam al-Hajj Ibrahim Niasse

All praise is due to Allah alone. May blessings and peace be upon he after whom there is no Prophet.

To proceed:

Questions have multiplied on whether it is possible, in accordance with he Sacred Law (Shariah), for the Muslims of the East and the West to be unified in the start and end of their fast and all their festivities. That is because they feel that they should be united. So, I composed this small work. Perhaps it will provide the answer. And in it, I am only transmitting. And trust should be given to the books from which I have copied. And Allah is the granter of success.

Allah (*Exalted is He*) has said: *"Indeed, the number of months with Allah are twelve in the Book of Allah on the day that He created the Heavens and the Earth"* [AL-TAWBAH, 36]. And He said: *"and He is the One who place the sun as a brilliant light and the moon as a splendor and the moon a light. And He decreed for it stages so that you may know and measure the number of years"* [YUNUS, 5]. And He said: *"Say: It is a measure of time for people and the Hajj"* [AL-BAQARAH, 189]. And He said: *"And We made the night and the day two signs. And We erased the sign of the night and made the sign of the day visible that you may seek the generosity of your Lord and so that you may know and measure the number of years"* [AL-ISRA, 12]. He also said: *"Fasting has been prescribed for you as it was prescribed for those before you, that you may be God-fearing. For a number of days"* [AL-BAQARAH, 183]. He also said: *"The month of Ramadan in which the Qur'an was revealed as a guidance for mankind and clear evidence of guidance and criterion. Thus, whoever among you witnesses the month, let him fast it"* [AL-BAQARAH, 185].

The exegete said it means, *"If anyone is present at the beginning of the month, then he should fast it."* Bukhari narrated from 'Abd Allah b. 'Umar that the Messenger of Allah (*may Allah bless him and give him peace*) said, *"The month is twenty-nine days. So, do not fast until you see it. If it is cloudy, then estimate it."* This narration is explained by the one in which he says, *"Then complete thirty days of Sha'ban."* It is further clarified by the explicit words of the Prophet (*may Allah bless him and give him peace*), as in al-Bukhari, *"We are an unlettered nation. We do not estimate or write. When you see it, fast. And when you see it, break your fast."*

What is clear is that if the *Ummah* begins to calculate and write, it will not affect the ruling of the Sacred Law under any circumstance. The author of *Muntaqi al-Akhbar*:

> Chapter on the *Hilal*: When it is seen by the people of one land, is it binding on the people of all the other lands?

> Kurayb said that Umm al-Fadl sent him to Mu'awiyah in Sham. *"So, I went to Sham and fulfilled her need. While in Sham, Ramadan came upon me. I saw the Hilal on a Thursday night. Then, I set out for Madinah at the end of the month. Abdullah b. 'Abbas asked me about the Hilal. He said, 'When did you all see the Hilal?' I said, 'We saw it on a Thursday night.' He asked, 'Did you see it?' I replied, 'Yes. And the people saw it. They and Mu'awiyah fasted.' He said, 'But we saw it on a Friday night. So, we will continue to fast until we complete it, or we see the Hilal.' I asked him, 'Is Mu'awiyah's sighting*

the moon and fasting not sufficient?' He replied, 'No. That is what the Messenger of Allah (may Allah bless him and give him peace) ordered us to do.'"

This was narrated by the authors of the six books except Bukhari and Ibn Majah. Al-Shawkani said in *Nayl al-Awtar*: The narrators doubted when he said, *"Is it not sufficient,"* whether he meant *"for us,"* or for Ibn 'Abbas. Those who said that the sighting of the moon in one land is not binding upon the people of another land were adhering to the Hadith of Kurayb. However, they were divided into different schools of thought regarding it. The author of *al-Fath* mentioned them: One group holds that each the inhabitants of every land should sight the moon, taking only into account their own sighting. The sighting of the moon in another land will not affect them. This opinion was transmitted by Ibn Mundhir from 'Ikrima, al-Qasim b. Muhammad, Salim and Ishaq. And it was transmitted as a solitary opinion of *"the people of knowledge."* It was also transmitted by al-Mawuridi as the opinion of the Shafi'is. The second opinion is that the sighting of the moon of the people of one land is not binding upon the people of another land, unless it is established by the Imam of the Muslims. That is because all the lands are as one with regard to him because his ruling is enacted upon all of them. This opinion was stated by Ibn al-Majishun. The third opinion is lands within the proximity of one another are under one moon sighting. If they are far away from one another, then there are two opinions. According to most of the scholars, the moonsighting in one land is not binding upon another land that is distant from it. That was transmitted by some of the Shafi'is. However, Abu al-Tayyib and a group of scholars opined that it is binding.

Al-Baghawi narrated various positions from Imam al-Shafi'i regarding the meaning of being distant. One of them it is having different horizons. This was the verdict of the Iraqis and al-Saydalani. And Nawawi declared it the correct position in *al-Rawdah* and *Sharh al-Madhhab*. The second having a distant border. This was the verdict of al-Baghawi. And al-Rafi'i and al-Nawawi declared this position as sound. The third is that they are distant if they are in different countries or districts. This position was transmitted in *al-Fath*.

The fourth position (on whether the moonsighting in one land is binding on another) is that it is binding upon everyone who would not be obstructed from seeing it, to the exclusion of all others. This position was transmitted from al-Sarkhasi. The fifth position is like the position of Ibn al-Majishun, mentioned above. The sixth position is that it is not binding when the two places differ in elevation, such as if one land is in a valley and the other in a mountain, or if each of the lands is in a different country. This was transmitted by al-Mahdi in al-Bahr, from Imam Yahya.

The guiding principle and the evidence for the people of all these opinions is this Hadith of Kurayb. And the way that proof is extracted from it is that Ibn 'Abbas did not act upon the sighting of the people of Sham and said, at the end of the Hadith, *"That is what the Messenger of Allah (may Allah bless him and give him peace) commanded us to do."* This statement indicated that he had memorized from the Messenger of Allah (*may Allah bless him and give him peace*) that it is not binding for the people of one land to follow the sighting of another land.

And you should know that the proof in the narration of Ibn 'Abbas is in that which he attributed to the Messenger of Allah (*may Allah bless him and give him peace*), rather than his juristic reasoning, which people understood from the narration. That attribution is what he indicated by saying, *"That is what the Messenger of Allah (may Allah bless him and give him peace) ordered us to do."* He was referring to his words, *"We will continue to fast until we complete thirty days..."* The order that came from the Messenger of Allah (*may Allah bless him and give him peace*) is what was narrated by Bukhari, Muslim and others, in the words, *"Do not fast until you see the hilal. And do not end your fast until you see it. If it is cloudy, complete the fast as thirty days."*

Such an order is not specific to a people or place in particular. Rather, it is addressed to every Muslim to which it applies. Thus, its being a proof for the binding nature of the moonsighting of one land over another land is more apparent than its being a proof for its not being binding because if one land has seen it, all the Muslims have seen it. So, that which was binding upon them would be binding upon everyone else.

If we were to submit that the words of Ibn 'Abbas indicate that the sighting of one land is not binding upon another land, its nonbinding nature would have to be specified by an intellectual proof, such being in distant quarters of the earth, which would make it nonbinding because they have different sunrises. In this case, Ibn 'Abbas not acting upon the sighting of the moon of the people of Sham, despite there not being such a great distance, was his own legal reasoning. And that is not a proof.

If we were to submit that its nonbinding nature is not specified by an intellectual proof, then no scholar doubts that the people of different, distant countries act upon each other's narrations. This is witnessed in all the rulings of the Sacred Law. And the sighting of the moon is one of those reasonings, whether in two distinct lands distant enough to allow for two sun rises or not. So, such a limitation is not acceptable without an evidence.

If we were to accept the soundness of this Hadith of Kurayb as evidence of the restriction, then it is imperative that it be restricted to that to which the statement refers, if the statement is known, or, if it is not known, upon the meaning of the statement. That is because it has come in opposition to analogical reason. Ibn 'Abbas did not mention the words of the Prophet (*may Allah bless him and give him peace*), nor their meaning, such that one could investigate what parts of it were universal and what parts were restricted. Rather, he brought an abstract statement that alluded to the reason as to why the people of Madinah did not act upon the sighting of the people of Sham.

Accepting that this is the meaning, without any additional

understood meaning that indicates it, such that we could make it restrictive to the universal principle in the Hadith, it would be necessary to restrict ourselves to what we understand from this text that contradicts analogical reasoning, without adding any other stipulations. As such, it would not be obligatory for the people of Madinah to act upon the sighting of the people of Sham. But such an exception would not apply to any of the other lands. And it is possible that there is something in the ruling that pertains to the people of Madinah that we do not understand.

If we were to accept the possibility of aggregate stipulations and restriction of the universal principle, the extent of the application of that restriction would be to places the distance between which is equal to or greater than that between Madinah and Sham. As for places that are closer to each other than Madinah to Sham, it would not apply. And this is evident.

Thus, it is imperative to investigate what evidence supports those who were of the opinion that one considers the country, region or land when considering whether to act upon a sight nor not. Rather, it is imperative to depend upon the opinion that was acted upon by the Malikis, a group of the Zaydis, including al-Mahdi, and what was transmitted by al-Qurtubi from his Shaykhs. That opinion is that when the people of one land see the moon, it is binding upon the people of every land. And no attention is to be paid to that which was said by Ibn 'Abd al-Barr that this opinion contradicts the consensus that a single sighting is not taken into account for two lands that are distant from each other, such as Khurasan and Andalus because such a consensus is not complete. This is evident because this group contradicts that opinion.

The text that was cited from *Fath al-Bari* on the explanation of the Hadith of Abdullah b. 'Umar, *"The month is twenty-nine days. So, do not fast until you see it...."* is as follows:

> The intended meaning does not tie the fast to every individual's sighting of the moon. Rather, the intending meaning is the sighting of a portion of the people, who are those who establish the beginning of the fast...

He continued until he said:

> The scholars have differed with each other, being divided into different schools of thought on the matter. One of them was of the opinion that the people of each land should sight the moon. This is supported by the Hadith from Sahih Muslim on the authority of Ibn 'Abbas. And it is the opinion transmitted by Ibn al-Mundhir from 'Ikrimah, al-Qasim, Salim and Ishaq. And al-Tirmidhi transmitted it as the solitary opinion of the people of knowledge. I twas also transmitted by al-Mawuridi who attributed it to al-Shafi'i.

> The second is the opposite of that opinion. It is that if the moon is sighted in one land, it is binding upon the people of every land. This is the preferred opinion among the Malikis. However, Ibn 'Abd al-Barr transmitted a consensus to the contrary. He said that there was consensus that a single sighting is not taken into account for two lands that are different, such as Khurasan and Andalus. Al-Qurtubi

said, *"Our Shaykhs have said that if the sighting of the hilal is undeniably apparent in one place, and news of it is transmitted to another place, with the testimony of two witnesses, it will be binding upon the latter place to fast also."* Ibn al-Majishun said, *"It is not binding upon them unless the witnesses are from the people of the land in which the sighting was established or unless it is established by the Imam of the Muslims. In that case, it is binding upon all people because the lands with regard to him are as one and his decree is enacted upon all."* Some of the Shafi'is said:

> If the lands are near, then the ruling will be singular. If they are far, then there two opinions. The majority say that it is not binding. And that is the opinion of Abu al-Tayyib. Another group says that it is binding. This opinion was transmitted by al-Baghawi on the authority of al-Shafi'i. Further, there is difference over what it meant by being distant. The first is that it if the horizons differ, such that the sunrise is different, they are distant. This was stated by the 'Iraqis and al-Saydalani. And Nawawi authenticated it in *al-Rawdah* and *Sharh al-Madhhab*. The second is that their borders be distant from one another. This was stated by the Imam and al-Baghawi. And al-Rafii authenticated it in *as-Saghir*. And al-Nawawi authenticated it in *Sharh Muslim*. The third is if they differ in altitude.

The fourth opinion [regarding the binding nature of the sighting] is that which was transmitted from al-Sarkhasi. He said, *"It is binding upon every land in which there is no obstruction to viewing it. But it is not binding upon others. The fifth is the opinion of Ibn al-Majishun, which we already mentioned. And others have used it as evidence that one who sights the hilal alone has to fast or break his fast, even if his word is not acted upon. This is the opinion of the four Imams regarding starting one's fast. However, they differed over this regarding ending one's fast. Al-Shafi'i said, 'He should end his fast and hide it.' The rest said that he should continue fasting out of caution."*

In *Tafsir al-Manar*, we find the following text:

Some have said that the meaning is *"Whoever among you that is present at the onset of the month, then let him fast it."* The Ustadh and Imam said, *"It was only said in this way, and He did not say, 'Then let them fast it' for the same wisdom for which the Qur'an did not establish the timings of the prayers."* That wisdom is that the Qur'an is the universal address of Allah to every human being. And He knows that there are places that have do not have normal days. Rather, nearly the entire year can be a day and a night, such as near the two poles. So, for example, the longitude where the South pole would have night for half the year and the North Pole would have day. And the days normalize according to the distance from the two poles, until at the equatorial line, the days and nights would be equal. Do you deem that Allah (*Exalted is He*) would charge someone who lives near or at one of the two equators with only praying five prayers, the first of them at the time of the rising of the dawn and the second after the sun moves from its zenith, etc., in a day that lasts a year or months at a time? Would he charge him to accurately fast Ramadan when he has no months at all, not to mention, Ramadan. Indeed, from the greatest signs that this Qur'an is from Allah whose knowledge encompasses all things, and that it is not written by a man, is what we see in it of limitation to universal address which is not restricted to the time and place of the one who brought it. If it had been from the Prophet (*may Allah bless him and give him peace*), all that it contains would correspond to the time and place in which he lived, and other, close places that he knew. And the Arabs didn't know that there were places on the earth in which a day and a night was equal to a month or a number of months according to our days and months. Thus, the Revealer of the Qur'an, who knows every hidden thing and the creator of the earth and the heavenly bodies, address all mankind in all of their possible states. Thus, He gave a general command to pray but the Messenger explained their times according to the situations of the lands where time passes normally, which are most of the lands on earth, so that when Islam would arrive to one of the lands that we indicated, it would be possible for the people of those lands to estimate the times of their prayers according to their legal reasoning, making analogy to what the Prophet (*may Allah bless him and give him peace*) had explained from the general command of Allah. It is the same for fasting. He only obligated Ramadan upon those who are witness the month and are present during it. For those who don't have a normal month like that of Ramadan, things are facilitated, and they may estimate its days. The jurists mentioned the issue of estimating only after they recognized that some lands' nights and days lengthened and shortened. And they differed over the manner of estimating regarding which land they should imitate. Some said that they should imitate the lands with moderate times, in which the Sacred Law was revealed, like Makkah and Madinah. Others said that they should estimate according to the closest of the lands with moderate times to them. Both are permissible because it is a matter of juristic reasoning with no text revealed regarding it.

In *Hashiyah al-Rahuni*, the author transmitted from al-Qarafi:

> Times differ from region to region. There is no zenith for any people except that it is Fajr, 'Asr, Maghrib or the middle of the night for others. Indeed, every time the sun moves a degree, it will be dawn, sunrise, zenith, sunset or midnight or midday and all the other names of the divisions of times, according to the differing regions. And Allah addressed every people with that which they could realize in their region. He did not make them have to experience the way that things are in other regions. So, [the Divine Speech] does not address anyone except with the timings that apply to his land. And that is agreed upon. Likewise, the appearance of the *hilal* differs. If it appears first in the West, it will not appear in the east until the second night because it is confined to the horizon. This is something that is necessarily known. The result of this foundational principle is that He addresses everyone according to the [sighting of] the *hilal* of his region. And he is not bound by the decree of any other region, even if it is mass transmitted. This is what was indicated by al-Bukhari when he said, *"Chapter: The people of every land should follow their own moonsighting."*

The following is mentioned in the same book:

> Mi'yar transmitted on the authority of al-Sa'igh, *"If someone obtains certain knowledge through associates, and they number more than four, fasting is binding upon him. That is the opinion of those who have verified the issue with our Shaykhs."* But al-Lakhami stated that it is not the number of witnesses that he considers when fasting. If they are not trustworthy, despite their number, their sighting is not binding upon anyone else. However, if he obtains knowledge that they are trustworthy, he fasts as long as there are not fewer than five witnesses.

Ibn al-'Arabi said in *al-Ahkam*:

> The seventh issue: If someone informs another about the sighting of the moon in one land, that land will inevitably be near or distant. If it is near, then the sighting of the moon is binding upon them. If it is far, there are two opinions. One group said that the people of each land must sight the moon. The others said that it would be binding upon them. In the Sahih, it is narrated from Kurayb that Umm al-Fadl sent him to Mu'awiyah b. Abi Sufyan in Sham. He said, *"So, I went to Sham and fulfilled her need. While I was there, the hilal of Ramadan appeared. I saw the hilal on a Thursday night. Then I returned to Madinah at the end of the month. Ibn 'Abbas asked me about the hilal, saying, 'When did you see it?' I said to him, 'I saw it on a Thursday night.' He said, 'But we only saw it on a Friday night.' I said to him, 'Is the sighting of Mu'awiyah not sufficient for you?' He replied, 'No. That is what the Messenger of Allah (may Allah bless him and*

give him peace) ordered us to do.'"

Scholars have differed over the interpretation of these words of Ibn 'Abbas. Some said that he rejected it because it was a solitary report. Others said that he rejected it because they are two regions with different horizons. The latter is the correct opinion because Kurayb was not giving testimony. Rather, he was only informing him of the ruling that was confirmed through witnessing. And there is no difference over the fact that a solitary report is sufficient to transmit a ruling established through witnessing. An example of this is if it the *hilal* was sighted on a Thursday night in Aghmat and in Seville on Friday night. Each land would go by their own sighting because Canopus is visible in Aghmat but not in Seville. And that is an indication of differing horizons.

And look at the issue that was raised on if the people of Basarah see the *hilal* of Ramadan and news of it reaches the people of Kufah, Madinah and Yemen. Ibn al-Qasim and Ibn Wahb narrated from Malik in *al-Majmu'ah* that the sighting is binding upon all of them. So, if they missed the fast, they should make it up. And Qadi Abu Ishaq narrated from Ibn al-Majishun that if the sighting is confirmed in Basarah by such a large group that it is not necessary to investigation and deliberation, then it is binding upon the people of every land. However, if it was only established through the testimony of two upright witnesses, then it is not binding upon other lands except in two cases. The first is that it is binding upon all the people of a land who are under the judge that issued the ruling. The second is that if it is established by the Muslim ruler, then it is binding upon all the Muslims. And that is the opinion of Malik. This was narrated in al-Muntaqi. And his words, *"binding upon all of them"* is referring to the people f the neighboring lands, as can be understood from the texts transmitted above.

'Allamah al-Hafiz Ibn Hajar al-'Asqalani said in *Subul al-Salam fi Sharh Bulugh al-Maram*:

> 'A'isha (*may Allah be pleased with her*) said, *"The Messenger of Allah (may Allah bless him and give him peace) said, 'The Day of the Feast [al-Fitr] is the day in which people feast. The Day of Sacrifice [al-Adha] is the day in which people sacrifice.'"* This was narrated by al-Tirmidh who said, *"This is a sound, solitary narration. Some of the people of knowledge explained this Hadith under the meaning that al-Fitr and fasting are with the collective and the majority of people."*

And it contains evidence that agreement between people is taken into account when confirming the *'Id* and that if someone sights the moon alone, he must corroborate with the congregation. And their ruling is binding upon him regarding the *'Id* prayer, ending the prayer and the sacrifice. Tirmidhi narrated a similar Hadith from Abu Hurayrah.

Al-Hasan said:

> This Hadith has the same meaning as the Hadith of Ibn 'Abbas qhen Kurayb said to him that the people of Sham and Mu'awiyah fasted after having seen the *hilal* on a Thursday night in Sham. Then he went to Madinah at the end of the month and informed Ibn 'Abbas of that. Ibn 'Abbas responded, *"But we saw it on a Friday night. So we will continue to fast until we complete thirty days or we see it."* He said, *"I responded,*

'Is it not sufficient for you that Mu'awiyah saw it along with the people?'" He said, *"No. The Messenger of Allah (may Allah bless him and give him peace) ordered us to do that."*

The apparent meaning of the Hadith is that Kurayb was one of the people who saw the moon. Yet, Ibn 'Abbas ordered him to complete his fast even if he was sure that it was the Day of 'Id. This was the opinion that Muhammad b. al-Hasan acted upon. He said, *"It is obligatory to act in congruence with mankind, even if it contradicts your own certainty. Likewise, it is obligatory to act upon this regarding the Hajj because it has come down that your 'Arafah is the day that you all know."*

However, the majority of scholars disagreed with that. They said, *"It is imperative to act upon one's certainty in one's personal actions."* They interpreted the Hadith as him never going against what the generality were upon. For, if afterwards it becomes clear that they made a mistake, what they acted upon had covered it over because the start and end are delayed for the one who is unsure. So, he had acted upon the fundamental principle.

They further explained that the Hadith ibn 'Abbas should be interpreted as his not having adhered to the sighting of the people of Sham because Sham and the Hijaz have different horizons. Further, the one who was informing him was a solitary witness. So, he did not act upon his testimony. There is nothing in it to indicate that he commanded Kurayb to act in contradiction to his personal conviction. He only informed him of the situation of the people of Madinah and that they had not known about the sighting in Sham for one of two reasons.

He also mentions in the same book [*Subul al-Salam*], after some discussion:

On this issue, there are many opinions. None of them have any definitive proof. The closest of them in correctness is that when the moon is sighted in one land, it is binding upon the lands that neighbor it in the same region. And in the words, *"when you see it,"* there is evidence that if a person sights the *hilal* alone, it is imperative that he fast and break his fast. Regarding beginning the fast, this is the opinion of the Imams of Ahl al-Bayt and the four Imams. But they differed over ending the fast. Al-Shafi'i said that he should end his fast and hide it. However, the majority said that he should continue to fast out of caution. That is what is recorded in *Al-Sharh*. However, it has already been mentioned in the first part of the Chapter on the Two '*Id* prayers, that no one opined that he should have abandoned his personal conviction and follow the ruling of people, except Muhammad b. al-Hasan al-Shaybani. And that the majority said that his personal conviction is binding upon him whenever he has certainty regarding the matter. So, what has been mentioned is insufficient evidence. And the reason for the disagreement is what Ibn 'Abbas said to Kurayb that he did not believe in the sighting of the *Hilal* while the latter was in Sham. Rather, he should go along with the people of Madinah, fasting thirty-one days according to the sighting of Sham, because it is thirty days according to the people of Madinah. And Ibn 'Abbas said that that was from the Sunnah. The hadith has already been mentioned. But it is not a textual evidence for that which they have tried to prove with it, because of the various possible meanings, as we have mentioned. So, the truth is that he should depend on his personal convictions in the beginning and the ending of the fast. And he should be careful of speaking on those convictions as a protection for the servants, to prevent them from having a bad opinion of him.

Thus, if someone investigates thoroughly the opinions of the Companions, the Tabi'in, the Imams, and the greatest scholars of the past and present, it will become evident to him that having a unified fast and breaking of the fast is a very difficult thing to do. In fact, even if we accept that one land should rely upon the sighting of another land, we receive news of the 'Id prayer happening in the Middle East while we have still not prayed the Fajr prayer. So, how would the matter be in the far east. Indeed, two years ago, I traveled to Hong Kong after midnight. I was aboard the plane for sixteen hours. I arrived in Beirut while the sun was rising, knowing that in my country of Senegal, it was clearly night. And in Hong Kong was already in the next night. And Allah is the One who grants success.

Peace,
Ibrahim Niasse

BIOGRAPHY OF THE AUTHOR

The following biography is based on "Shaykh Ibrahim Niasse: Revivalist of the Sunnah," a paper presented by Shaykh Hassan Cisse to a Northwestern University conference on Muslim Scholars in Africa (1984).

Shaykh Ibrahim Niasse (1900-1975) was West Africa's most renowned Islamic scholar in the twentieth century. His followers numbered in the millions and comprised the largest single Muslim movement in West Africa (Hiskett, 1984). He was also well-known among the *ulama* and leaders of the broader Muslim world and a member of such organizations as the Muslim World League (*Rabitat al-'Alam al-Islami* based in Saudi Arabia, of which he served as Vice President), the World Muslim Congress (*Mutamar al-'Alam al-Islami*; Karachi, Pakistan), the Islamic Research Assembly (*Majma' al-Buhuth al-Islamiyya*; Egypt) and the High Council of Islamic Affairs (*Majlis al-'Ala li al-Shu'un al-Islamiyya*; Egypt). Following a trip to Cairo, Egypt, in 1961, he became widely known as *Shaykh al-Islam* after having led the Friday prayers in the prestigious Azhar mosque.

Shaykh Ibrahim also maintained close relations with several prominent leaders in the independence movements during the 1960s, such as Kwame Nkrumah (Ghana), Ahmad Sekou Touré (Guinea) and Gamal Abd al-Nasser (Egypt). He campaigned tirelessly for governments to respect the rights of Muslims and the oppressed worldwide. He spoke out on several international causes, such as Israeli aggression toward the Palestinians, but he was also interested in interfaith issues and maintained good relations with Vatican representatives. He also became involved in social concerns, stressing racial equality and the rights of women. In regards to the latter, the Shaykh encouraged women to *"compete with men in knowledge."*

Shaykh Ibrahim Abdullah Niasse was born in rural Senegal, the son al-Hajj Abdullah Muhammad Niasse. Al-Hajj Abdullah (d. 1922) represented the culmination of a long line of Islamic scholars in the Senegambia region, and was himself a well-traveled and consummate shaykh, attracting students from all around the region as far away as Mauritania. Shaykh Ibrahim was educated primarily at the hands of his father, with full access to his father's extensive library. Shaykh Ibrahim mastered at an early age from his father the full range of Islamic sciences: the Qur'an and its interpretation, the Hadith and their explanation, jurisprudence and Sufism.

In reference to his educational background and achievements, Shaykh Ibrahim said, *"I learned Qur'an and Hadith first from my shaykh, my father, and he, from his father. I received an 'ijaza (diploma from the majalis al-'ilm) first from my father in both Qur'an and Hadith, then from Abdur-Rahman b. al-Hajj al-'Alawi (Mauritania) and another 'ijaza from Shaykh Ahmad Sukayrij (Morocco) who himself had earned some six hundred 'ijazas from six hundred different shaykhs whose names are mentioned in his book, where he writes, 'The first one to whom I gave authorization in all these chains of transmission was the Khalifa al-Hajj Ibrahim Niasse.'"* Shaykh Ibrahim once said concerning his scholarly credentials: *"What I have in the way of 'ijaza and muqaddam authorizations would indeed fill a book."*

As for the content of his teaching, it was nothing more or less than the Qur'an and the Sunnah of the Prophet Muhammad and its revitalization. Throughout his life, the example of the Prophet was his means and end. Shaykh Ibrahim used to say, *"If the best of mankind, the Prophet is moving, even I shall follow him step by step; and the day he stops from there I shall never move."* Elsewhere in a poem, Shaykh Ibrahim wrote, *"If I am asked, what is your madhhab (school of jurisprudence) and who is your beloved, I can answer that it the Prophet, and none other."*

Shaykh Ibrahim was the best example of a Sufi according to the description *"The Sufi is the son of his hour (ibn waqtihi)."* He will respond to the needs of the time. At every moment he is dealing with the requirements of that moment. The Muslim who is greatest in understanding is he who submits to the rule of his hour. That is, he gives everything the position it requires in action and speech. He is a person moving with time in a circle. He does not attempt to stop time, not to become stagnant in it, nor to regress in it. His effort is aimed at continually moving forward. In the season of Ramadan he reads Qur'an and Hadith and presents their explanations. In the season of Hajj, he expounds the virtues of the Muslim pilgrimage. At the time of *Mawlid*, he recites the Prophet's Sira or Biography.

All of this behavior characterized the Sufism of Shaykh Ibrahim. It was based on action and practice, traveling all over the Muslim world, giving speeches, writing pamphlets. In every endeavor, his goal was to direct Muslims to the right path (*siratul mustaqim*). Sickness did not bother him unless it halted his activity in behalf of spreading Islam. Indeed, his *tasawwuf* was not characterized by heedlessness and neglect (*ghafla*). It was based on real Islam, mastering the self (*nafs*) and ruling over it with Qur'an and Sunnah. His Sufism was producing and working in various fields of life on the farms, and so forth.

In a speech in the 1960s, Shaykh Ibrahim addressed a group of Muslim youth and said, *"For the youth, I thank you all for your papers. And I am here to tell you to go ahead and be in the vanguard of things. Surely the future of every nation is based on its youth. But it is not based upon all of them, not upon every individual, but only on the intellectual ones, the educated ones with good character, good manners, and zeal. As for the youth lacking education and good character, he is like a seed unfertilized. So make every effort to seek and do your best to acquire more knowledge, not only Islamic knowledge, not only mathematics and its branches, but also be part of and cooperate with those whose zeal is to discover the unknown and unseen things of this world."*

Throughout his life, Shaykh Ibrahim's character was based on the Qur'an and the Sunnah of the Prophet, a fact verified by prominent Muslim leaders who knew him. For example, we note in the letter of Shaykh Muhammad al-Hafiz al-Tijani—the Egyptian who was known as the foremost man of Hadith in his age—the words:

"Praise belongs to Allah, after Allah has blessed us by binding us in love: this humble servant Muhammad al-Hafiz al-Tijani and the Hujja, the cornerstone of the religion, the sea of confidence, the believer in Allah, my brother and the brother of my spirit, my master Abi Ishaq, Shaykh Ibrahim ...."

In his greeting, it is important to note that Shaykh al-Hafiz uses the word *Hujja*, or "the proof", as a form of address. The scholars of hadith have ranked the scholars who work in this field. Each rank has a specific name. For example, the *muhaddith* is the narrator of hadith who reads traditions based upon narration and report.

The *hafiz* has memorized hadith to the number of one hundred thousand along with their explanation. But the *Hujja* has memorized three hundred thousand hadith with their explanations and chains of transmission from the Prophet. Likewise, a 1961 letter from the Secretary General of the Muslim World League in Mecca, the late Shaykh Muhammad Surui al-Sabban, addresses Shaykh Ibrahim as follows:

"The Owner of Virtue, The Member of the Islamic Conference, Brother Shaykh Ibrahim Niasse well-respected, Assalamu Alaikum. Peace be upon you, and the mercy of Allah, and His Blessing be upon you. The pioneers have left the Hijaz, along with the propagators of the religion. They also left with the jurisprudence/understanding (fiqh) of the Hijaz, and now it remains with you, Shaykh Ibrahim. The old style of reading the Qur'an has also left the Hijaz, but you have remained reading the word of Allah with this same style of Hijaz, the style of Nafi Mawla Abi Nu'aym. Indeed, you are of the real people of Medina in both Fiqh and Qur'an. These are the proofs of your steadfastness, and it is not the pride from within me, but the pride is for you and by Him. You have believed and steadfastly you have protected and spread the religion and become victorious."

Tijani.org

وأئمة المذاهب الأربعة في الصوم واختلفوا في الإفطار فقال الشافعي يفطر ويخفيه وقال الأكثر يستمر صائما احتياطا كذا قاله في الشرح ولكنه تقدم له في أول باب صلاة العيدين أنه لم يقل بأنه يترك يقين نفسه ويتابع حكم الناس إلا محمد بن الحسن الشيباني وأن الجمهور يقولون أنه يتعين عليه حكم نفسه فيما يتيقنه فناقض هنا ما سلف وسبب الخلاف قول ابن عباس لكريب أنه لا يعتقد برؤية الهلال وهو بالشام بل يوافق أهل المدينة فيصوم الحادي والثلاثين باعتبار رؤية الشام لأنه يوم الثلاثين عند أهل المدينة وقال ابن عباس أن ذلك من السنة وتقدم الحديث وليس فيما بنص احتجوا به لاحتماله له كما تقدم فالحق أنه يمل بيقين نفسه صوما وافطارا ويحسن التكلم بهما صونا للعباد عن إثمهم بإساءة الظن به. اهـ

فمن أمعن النظر في أقوال الصحابة والتابعين وأقوال الأئمة وأجلاء العلماء من المتقدمين والمتأخرين يبدوا له جليا أن توحيد الصيام والإفطار من الصعوبة بمكان حتى لو سلمنا إعتماد بلد على رؤية بلد فإننا نسمع صلاة العيد في الشرق الأوسط فقط ونحن لم نصلي الصبح بعد فكيف بالأمر في الشرق الأقصى فإني منذ عامين رحلت من عنكوك (هونج كونج) بعد منتصف الليل وواصلت الطيران لمدة ستة عشرة ساعة وحللت ببيروت عند طلوع الشمس وأنا أعلم أن بلدي سنغال في الليلة البارحة وعنكوك (هونج كونج) في الليلة القابلة والله ولي التوفيق.. والسلام.

ابراهيم نياس

الموافقة للناس وأن المنفرد بمعرفة يوم العيد بالرؤية يجب عليه موافقة غيره ويلزمه حكمهم في الصلاة والإفطار والأضحية وقد أخرج الترمذي مثل هذا الحديث عن ابن هريرة وقال الحسن في معناه حديث ابن عباس وقد قال له كريب انه صام أهل الشام ومعاوية برؤية الهلال يوم الجمعة بالشام وقدم المدينة آخر الشهر وأخبر ابن العباس بذلك فقال ابن عباس لاكنا رأيناه ليلة السبت فلا نزال نصوم حتى نكمل ثلاثين أو نراه قال قلت أو لا تكتفي برؤية معاوية والناس قال لا هكذا أمرنا رسول الله ﷺ وظاهر الحديث أن كريبا ممن رآه وأنه أمره ابن العباس أن يتم صومه وإن كان متيقنا أنه يوم عيد وذهب إلى هذا محمد بن الحسن وقال يجب موافقة الناس وإن خالف يقين نفسه وكذا في الحج لأنه ورد وعرفتكم يوم تعرفون وخالفه الجمهور وقالوا إنه يجب عليه العمل في نفسه بما تيقنه وحملوا الحديث على عدم معرفته بما يخالف الناس فإنه إذا إنكشف بعد الخطأ فقد أجزاه ما فعله قالوا وتأخر الأيام في حق من التبس عليه وعمل بالأصل وتأولوا حديث ابن عباس بأنه يحتمل أنه لم يقل برؤية أهل الشام لاختلاف المطالع في الشام والحجاز وأنه لما كان المخبر واحد لم يعمل بشهادته وليس فيه أنه أمر كريبا بالعمل بخلاف يقين نفسه فإنما أخبر عن أهل المدينة وأنهم لا يعملون بذلك لأحد الأمرين. اهـ وفيه أيضا بعد كلام تقدم ذكره ما نصه وفي المسألة أقوال ليس على أحدها دليل ناهض والأقرب لزوم أهل بلد الرؤية وما يتصل بها من الجهات التي على سمتها وفي قوله لرؤيته دليل على أن الواحد إذا انفرد برؤية الهلال لزمه الصوم والإفطار وهو قول أئمة الآل

كريب لم يشهد وإنما أخبر عن حكم ثبت بشهادة ولا خلاف في أن الحكم الثابت بالشهادة يجري فيه خبر الواحد ونظيره ما لو ثبت أنه أهل ليلة الجمعة بأغمات وأهل بإشبيلية ليلة السبت فيكون لأهل كل بلد رؤيتهم لأن سهيلا يكشف من أغمات ولا يكشف من إشبيلية وهذا يدل على اختلاف المطالع. اهـ منه.

أنظر مسألة وإذا رأى أهل البصرة هلال رمضان ثم بلغ ذلك أهل الكوفة والمدينة واليمن فالذي رواه ابن القاسم وابن وهب عن مالك في المجموعة لزمهم الصيام أو القضاء إن فات الأداء، وروى القاضي أبو إسحاق عن ابن الماجشون أنه إن كان ثبت بالبصرة بأمر شائع ذائع يستغني عن الشهرة والتعديل فإنه يلزم غيرهم من أهل البلاد القضاء وإن كان إنما ثبت عندهم بشهادة شاهدين عدلين لم يلزم ذلك من البلاد الا من كان يلزمه حكم ذلك الحاكم ممن هو في ولايته أو يكون ذلك يثبت عند أمير المؤمنين فيلزم القضاء جماعة المسلمين، قال وهذا قول مالك. اهـ المنتقى. وقوله من أهل البلاد يعني المجاورة له كما فهم مما تقدم من النقول.

وفي سبل السلام في شرح بلوغ المرام للعلامة الحافظ بن حجر العسقلاني ما نصه : عن عائشة رضي الله عنها قالت قال رسول الله ﷺ الفطر يوم يفطر الناس والأضحى يوم يضحي الناس رواه الترمذي وقال بعد سياقه هذا حديث حسن غريب. وفسر بعض أهل العلم هذا الحديث أن معنى هذا الفطر والصوم مع الجماعة ومعظم الناس. اهـ بلفظه فيه دليل على أنه يعتبر في ثبوت العيد

وهذا معلوم بالضرورة ومقتضى القاعدة أن يخاطب كل أحد بهلال قطره ولا يلزمه حكم غيره ولو ثبت بالطرق القاطعة وإلى هذا أشار البخاري بقوله باب لكل أهل بلد رؤيتهم. اهـ

وفيه أيضا ما نصه المعيار عن الصائغ فمن وقع له العلم الضروري بقول أهل الرفقة أو بقول من كان أكثر من الأربعة لزمه الصوم هذا قول من حقق النظر من شيوخنا. اهـ منه بلفظه ونصه عن اللخمي ليس لعدد من يصام بشهادته إذا كان غير عدل أمر محصور لا يتعدى إلا أنه متى وقع العلم بصدقهم صام ما لم يكن أقل من خمسة. أهـ منه بلفظه.

وفي الأحكام لابن العربي مانصه :

المسألة السابعة إذا أخبر مخبر عن رؤية بلد فلا يخلو أن يقرب أو يبعد فإن قرب فالحكم واحد وإن بعد فقد قال قوم لأهل كل بلد رؤيتهم وقيل يلزمهم ذلك وفي الصحيح عن كريب أن أم الفضل بعثته إلى معاوية بن أبي سفيان بالشام قال فقدمت الشام فقضيت حاجتها واستهل علي هلال رمضان وأنا بالشام قال فقدمت الشام فقضيت حاجتها واستهل علي هلال رمضان وأنا بالشام فرأيت الهلال ليلة الجمعة ثم قدمت المدينة في آخر الشهر فسألني ابن عباس ثم ذكر الهلال فقال متى رأيته فقلت ليلة الجمعة قال لاكنا رأيناه ليلة السبت فقلت له أو لا تكتفي برؤية معاوية قال لا هكذا أمرنا رسول الله ﷺ واختلف في تأويل قول ابن عباس هذا فقيل ردّه لأنه خبر واحد وقيل ردّه لأن الأقطار مختلفة في المطالع وهو الصحيح لأن

أو أشهر من أنهارنا وأشهرنا، ولياليها كذلك، فمنزل القرآن وهو علام الغيوب وخالق الأرض والأفلاك خاطب الناس كافة بما يمكن أن يمتثلوه فأطلق الأمر بالصلاة والرسول بين أوقاتها بما يناسب حال البلاد المعتدلة التي هي القسم الأعظم من الأرض حتى إذا وصل الإسلام إلى أهل البلاد التي أشرنا إليها يمكنهم أن يقدروا للصلوات باجتهادهم والقياس على ما بينه النبي ﷺ من أمر الله المطلق، وكذلك الصيام. ما أوجب رمضان إلا على من شهد الشهر وحضره والذين ليس لهم شهر مثله يسهل عليهم أن يقدروا له قدره وقد ذكر الفقهاء مسئلة التقدير بعدما عرفوا بعض البلاد التي يطول ليلها ويقصر نهارها والبلاد التي يطول نهارها ويقصر ليلها واختلفوا في التقدير على أي البلاد يكون، فقيل على البلاد المعتدلة التي وقع فيها التشريع كمكة والمدينة، وقيل على أقرب بلاد معتدلة إليهم وكل منهما جائز فإنه اجتهادي لا نص فيه. اهـ.

وفي حاشية الرهوني نقلا عن القرافي ما نصه أن الأوقات تختلف بحسب الأقطار فما من زوال لقوم إلا وهو فجر وعصر ومغرب ونصف ليل لآخرين بل كلما تحركت الشمس درجة كانت فجرا وطلوع شمس وزوالا وغروبا ونصف ليل ونهار وسائر أسماء الزمان تنتسب إليها بحسب أقطار مختلفة، وخاطب الله كل قوم بما يتحققون في قطرهم لا في قطر غيرهم فلا يخاطب أحد بغير زوال بلده ولا بفجره وهذا مجمع عليه، وكذلك الهلال مطالعه مختلفة فيظهر في المغرب ولا يظهر في المشرق إلى الليلة الثانية لاحتباسه في الشعاع

ـــ خامسها قول ابن الماجشون المتقدم واستدل به على وجوب الصوم والفطر على من رأى الهلال وحده وإن لم يثبت قوله وهو قول الأئمة الأربعة في الصوم واختلفوا في الفطر فقال الشافعي يفطر ويخفيه وقال الأكثر يستمر صائما إحتياطا. اهـ

وفي تفسير المنار ما نصه وقال بعضهم إن المعنى فمن كان حاضرا منكم حلول الشهر فليصمه قال الأستاذ الإمام وإنما عبر بهذه العبارة ولم يقل فصوموه لمثل الحكمة التي لم يحدد القرآن مواقيت الصلاة لأجلها وذلك أن القرآن خطاب الله العام لجميع البشر وهو يعلم أن المواقع ما لا شهور فيها ولا أيام معتدلة بل السنة كلها قد تكون فيها يوما وليلة تقريبا كالجهات القطبية فالمدة التي يكون فيها القطب الشمالي في ليل وهي نصف السنة ويكون القطب الجنوبي والبعد عن القطبين ويستويان في خط الإستواء وهو وسط الأرض، أرأيت هل يكلف الله تعالى من يقيم في جهة القطبين وما يقرب منها أن يصلي في يومه وهو سنة أو مقدار عدة أشهر خمس صلوات إحداها حين يطلع الفجر والثانية بعد زوال الشمس... الخ، ويكلفه أن يصوم شهر رمضان بالتعيين ولا رمضان له ولا شهور، كلا إن من الآيات الكبرى على كون هذا القرآن من عند الله المحيط علمه بكل شيء لا من تأليف البشر ما نراه فيه من الإكتفاء بالخطاب العالم الذي لا يتقيد بزمان من جاء به ولا مكانه ولو كان من عند النبي ﷺ لكان كل ما فيه مناسبا لحال زمانه وبلاده وما يليها من البلاد التي يعرفها ولم تكن العرب تعرف أن في الأرض بلادا نهارها كعدة أشهر

ابن عباس ما يشهد له وحكاه ابن المنذر عن عكرمة والقاسم وسالم وإسحاق وحكاه الترمذي عن أهل العلم ولم يحك سواه وحكاه الماوردي وجها للشافعية ؛

ثانيها : مقابله إذا رؤي ببلدة لزم أهل البلاد كلها وهو المشهور عند المالكية لكن حكى ابن عبد البر الإجماع على خلافه وقد أجمعوا على أنه لا تراعى الرؤية فيما بعد من البلاد كخراسان والأندلس، قال القرطبي قد قال شيوخنا إذا كانت رؤية الهلال ظاهرة قاطعة بموضع ثم نقل إلى غيرهم بشهادة إثنين لزمهم الصوم وقال ابن الماجشون لا يلزمهم بالشهادة إلا أهل البلد الذي ثبتت فيه الشهادة إلا أن يثبت عند الإمام الأعظم فيلزم الناس كلهم لأن البلاد في حقه كالبلد الواحد إذ حكمه نافذ في الجميع وقال بعض الشافعية إن تقاربت البلاد كان الحكم واحداً وإن تباعدت فوجهان لا يجب عند الأكثر واختار أبو الطيب وطائفة الوجوب وحكاه البغوي عن الشافعي وفي ضبط البعد أوجه :

— أحدها إختلاف المطالع، قطع به العراقيون والصيدلاني وصححه النووي في الروضة وشرح المهذب ؛

— ثانيها مسافة القطر، قطع به الإمام والبغوي وصححه الرافعي في الصغير والنووي في شرح مسلم ؛

— ثالثها اختلاف الأقاليم ؛

— رابعها حكاه السرخسي فقال يلزم كل بلد لا يتصور خفاؤه عنهم بلا عارض دون غيرهم ؛

عمومه وخصوصه إنما جاءنا بصيغة مجملة أشار بها إلى قصة هي عدم عمل أهل المدينة برؤية أهل الشام على تسليم أن ذلك المراد ولم نفهم منه زيادة على ذلك حتى نجعله مخصصا لذلك العموم فينبغي الإقتصار على المفهوم من ذلك الوارد على خلاف القياس وعدم الإلحاق به فلا يجب على أهل المدينة العمل برؤية أهل الشام دون غيرهم ويمكن أن يكون ذلك في حكمه لا نعقلها ولو نسلم صحة الإلحاق وتخصيص العموم به فغايته أن يكون في المحلات التي بينها من البعد مابين المدينة والشام أو أكثر وأما في أقل من ذلك فلا وهذا ظاهر فينبغي أن ينظر ما دليل من ذهب إلى إعتبار البريد أو الناحية أو البلد في المنع من العمل بالرؤية والذي ينبغي إعتماده هو ما ذهب إليه المالكية وجماعة من الزيدية واختاره المهدي منهم وحكاه القرطبي عن شيوخه أنه إذا رءاه أهل بلد لزم أهل البلاد كلها ولا يلتفت إلى ما قاله ابن عبد البر من أن هذا القول خلاف الإجماع قال لأنهم قد أجمعوا على أنه لا تراعى الرؤية فيما بعد من البلدان كخراسان والأندلس وذلك لأن الإجماع لا يتم وانخالف مثل هؤلاء الجماعة. اه، ونص ما في فتح الباري شرح البخاري في شرح حديث عبد الله بن عمر الشهر تسع وعشرون فلا تصوموا حتى تروه ما نصه ليس المراد تعليق الصوم بالرؤية في حق كل أحد بل المراد بذلك رؤية بعضهم وهو من يثبت به ذلك إلى أن قال وقد اختلف العلماء في ذلك على مذاهب ؛

أحدها : لأهل كل بلد رؤيتهم، وفي صحيح مسلم من حديث

واعلم أن الحجة إنما هي في المرجوع من رواية إبن عباس لا في اجتهاده الذي فهم عنه الناس والمشار إليه بقوله هكذا أمرنا رسول الله ﷺ : هو قوله فلا نزال نصوم حتى نكمل الثلاثين والأمر الكائن من رسول الله ﷺ هو ما أخرجه الشيخان وغيرهما بلفظ لا تصوموا حتى تروا الهلال ولا تفطروا حتى تروه فإن غُمّ عليكم فاكملوا العدة ثلاثين، وهذا لا يختص بأهل ناحية على وجهة الإنفراد بل هو خطاب لكل من يصلح له من المسلمين، فالإستدلال به على لزوم رؤية أهل بلد لغيرهم من البلاد أظهر من الإستدلال به على عدم اللزوم لأنه إذا رءاه أهل بلد فقد رآه المسلمون فيلزم غيرهم مالزمهم ولو سلم توجه الإشارة في كلام إبن عباس إلى عدم لزوم رؤية أهل بلد لأهل بلد آخر لكان عدم اللزوم مقيدا بدليل العقل وهو أن يكون بين القطرين من البعد ما يجوز معه لإختلاف المطالع وعدم عمل إبن عباس برؤية أهل الشام مع عدم البعد الذي يمكن معه الإختلاف عمل بالاجتهاد وليس بحجة ولو سلم عدم لزوم التقييد بالعقل فلا يشك عالم أن الأدلة قاضية بأن أهل الأقطار يعمل بعضهم بخبر بعض وشهادته في جميع الأحكام الشرعية والرؤية من جملتها وسواء كان بين القطرين من البعد ما يجوز معه إختلاف المطالع أم لا فلا يقبل التخصيص إلا بدليل ولو سلم صلاحية حديث كريب هذا للتخصيص فينبغي أن يقتصر على محل النص إن كان النص معلوما أو على المفهوم منه إن لم يكن معلوما لوروده على خلاف القياس ولم يأت إبن عباس لفظ النبي ﷺ ولا بمعنى لفظه حتى ننظر في

مذاهب ذكرها صاحب الفتح : أحدها أنه يعتبر لأهل كل بلد رؤيتهم ولا يلزمهم رؤية غيرهم حكاه ابن المنذر عن عكرمة والقاسم ابن محمد وسالم وإسحاق وحكاه الترمذي عن أهل العلم ولم يحك سواه وحكاه الماوردي وجها للشافعية ؛ وثانيا أنه لا يلزم أهل البلد رؤية غيرهم إلا أن يثبت ذلك عند الإمام الأعظم فيلزم الناس كلهم لأن البلد في حقه كالبلد الواحد إذ حكمه نافذ في الجميع. قاله ابن الماجشون ؛ وثالثا أنها إن تقاربت البلاد كان الحكم واحداً وإن تباعدت فوجهان لا يجب عند الأكثر، قاله بعض الشافعية واختار أبو الطيب وطائفة الوجوب وحكاه البغوي عن الشافعي في ضبط البعد أوجه أحدها إختلاف المطالع قطع بها العراقيون والصيدلاني وصححه النووي في الروضة وشرح المذهب ثانيها مسافة القطر قطع به البغوي وصححه الرافعي والنووي ثالثها باختلاف الأقاليم حكاه في الفتح رابعها أنه يلزم أهل كل بلد لا يتصور خفاؤه عنهم بلا عارض دون غيرهم حكاه السرخسي خامسها مثل قول إبن الماجشون المتقدم سادسها أنه لا يلزم إذا إختلفت الجهتان إرتفاعا وإنحدارا كان يكون أحدهما سهلا والآخر جبلا أو كان كل بلد في إقليم، حكاه المهدي في البحر عن الإمام يحيى والهادوية وحجة أهل هذه الأقوال حديث كريب هذا ووجه الإحتجاج به أن إبن عباس لم يعمل برؤية أهل الشام وقال في آخر الحديث هكذا أمرنا رسول الله ﷺ، فدلّ ذلك على أنه قد حفظ من رسول الله ﷺ أنه لا يلزم أهل بلد العمل برؤية أهل بلد آخر.

قال المفسر فمن كان حاضرا منكم حلول الشهر فليصمه. وقد أخرج البخاري عن عبد الله بن عمر أن رسول الله ﷺ قال : الشهر تسع وعشرون فلا تصوموا حتى تروه فإن غم عليكم فاقدروا له. وهذا يفسره رواية فاكملوا عدة شعبان ثلاثين ويزيده ايضاحا تصريح النبيَّ ﷺ. وهو كما في البخاري : «إنا أمة أمية لا نحسب ولا نكتب إذا رأيتموه فصوموا وأذار أيتموه فأفطروا» الحديث. ومن الواضح أن الأمة إذا أمست تحسب وتكتب فلن يغيَر ذلك الحكم الشرعي بحال من الأحوال، قال في منتقى الأخبار (   ) باب الهلال : إذا رآه أهل بلد هل يلزم بقية البلاد ؟ عن كريب : أن أم الفضل بعثته إلى معاوية بالشام فقال فقدمت الشام فقضيت حاجتها واستهل عليَ رمضان وأنا بالشام فرأيت الهلال ليلة الجمعة ثم قدمت المدينة في آخر الشهر فسألني عبد الله بن عباس ثم ذكر الهلال فقال متى رأيتهم الهلال فقلت رأيناه ليلة الجمعة فقال أنت رأيته فقلت نعم ورآه الناس وصاموا وصام معاوية فقال لا كنا رأيناه ليلة السبت فلا نزال نصوم حتى نكمل أو نراه. فقلت ألا تكتفي برؤية معاوية وصيامه ؟ فقال لا هكذا أمرنا رسول الله ﷺ. رواه الجماعة إلا البخاري وإبن ماجة. قال الشوكاني في نيل الأوطار : قوله واستهل عليَ رمضان هو بضم التاء من إستهل قاله النووي. قوله : أفلا تكتفي شك أحد رواته هل هو بالخطاب لا إبن عباس أو بنون اجمع للمتكلم. وقد تمسك بحديث كريب هذا من قال أنه لا يلزم أهل بلد رؤية أهل بلد غيرها، وقد إختلوا في ذلك على

بحث في ثبوت الهلال

بقلم فضيلة شيخ الإسلام الحاج إبراهيم نياس

الحمد لله وحده والصلاة والسلام على من لا نبي بعده

أما بعد :

فقد كثر السؤال عما إذا كان من الممكن توحيد صيام المسلمين وإفطارهم وسائر أعيادهم في مشارق الأرض ومغاربها، من قبل الحكم الشرعي لكون ذلك ربما يدعوا إلى شعورهم بوحدتهم فقيدت هذه العجالة عسى أن يتضمن الجواب وليس لي فيها إلا مجرد النقل فالعهدة على الكتب المنقول منها والله ولي التوفيق.

قال الله تعالى : ﴿إن عدة الشهور عند الله إثنى عشر شهرا في كتاب الله يوم خلق السماوات والأرض﴾ وقال : ﴿وهو الذي جعل الشمس ضياء والقمر نورا وقدره منازل لتعلموا عدد السنين والحساب﴾، وقال : ﴿قل هي مواقيت للناس والحج﴾، وقال : ﴿وجعلنا الليل والنهار آيتين فمحونا آية الليل وجعلنا آية النهار مبصرة لتبتغوا فضلا من ربكم ولتعلموا عدد السنين والحساب﴾، وقال : ﴿كتب عليكم الصيام كما كتب على الذين من قبلكم لعلكم تتقون أياما معدودات﴾، ثم قال : ﴿شهر رمضان الذي أنزل فيه القرآن هدى للناس وبينات من الهدى والفرقان فمن شهد منكم الشهر فليصمه﴾.

www.ingramcontent.com/pod-product-compliance
Lightning Source LLC
Chambersburg PA
CBHW060344080526
44584CB00013B/910